D0734358

The
Miseries
of
Human Life

The Miseries of Human Life

By James Beresford, adapted by Michelle Lovric
Designed by AB3 and Michelle Lovric
Copyright © 1995 Michelle Lovric,
Covent Garden, London
Produced by Imago
Manufactured in China
Technical Editor: Brian Burns
Cover illustration by George Cruikshank
Calligraphy by Alan Peacock

First published in Great Britain by PAST TIMES, Oxford, England.
0 9 8 7 6 5 4 3 2 1

Acknowledgements

The editor gratefully acknowledges the assistance of the following people:
Kristina Blagojevitch, Nicola Carr, Karen Hayes, Eleanor Knight,
Melissa Lovric, Wendy and Fred Oliver.
With special thanks to Dr Bruce Barker-Benfield
at the Bodleian Library, Oxford, for his advice and help.

The Miseries Of Human Life

by James Beresford,
adapted by Michelle Lovric

PAST TIMES™

Hei mihi!	Virg. AEn. II.–274.
Ditto.	Ditto Ditto XII.–620.
Ditto.	Prop. Lib. IV. Eleg. I.–58.
Heu!	Virg. Geor. Lib. IV. –491. et passim
Heu, Heu!	Catul. Poem. LXXX.–6.
Proh dolor!	Tit. Liv.
Oime!	Guarini. Past. Fido, Atto second. Scen. sesta.
Me miserable!	Milt. Par. Lost. B.IV.—73.
Alas!	Shak. Milt. &c., &c., &c. passim.
Oh! oh! oh!	Shak. Macb. Act V. Scene 1.
O! O! O!	Ditto Othel. Act V. Scene 1
O! O! O!	Ditto. Ditto. Ditto. Ditto.
Ah me!	Eng. Trag. passim.
Helas!	Fr. Ditto. Ditto.

Contents

Editor's Note.. page 6

Miseries Personal,
Existential and of the Body.................. page 8

Miseries of the Table .... page 14

Miseries Domestic, including the
Dressing Room and Bed-Chamber....... page 21

Miseries of Travelling .... page 27

Miseries of Social Life .... page 33

Miseries of the Country, including
Country Walks and Gardens.................. page 42

Miseries of the Town .... page 47

Miseries of Watering Places.................. page 51

Miseries of Fashionable Life.................. page 55

Miseries of Reading
    and Writing .... page 61

EDITOR'S NOTE

In early 1806, James Beresford, an English rector, published *The Miseries of Human Life*. The book listed, in excruciating detail, and with the utmost elegance of expression, the multitude of petty outrages, minor humiliations and tiny discomforts that make up everyday human existence. Beresford arranged his pageant of calamities in a series of "Groans" — about the body, about travelling, about social life, about life in town and life in the country, amongst other unspeakable horrors. *Miseries* was an instant sensation, an immediate best-seller and was even praised by Sir Walter Scott for its "wit, ... humour and perfect originality".

The *Miseries* were based on a series of discussions between a Mr Samuel Sensitive and a Mr Timothy Testy, both martyrs to their nerves and tender prey to all the injuries, insults, disappointments and treacheries — "that family of Mental Mortifications" — which afflict the sentient and the sensitive on a daily basis. Their theory is that the sheer tonnage of the small Miseries of life actually exceeds in direness the effects of those larger, more glamorous catastrophes, such as shipwreck, hurricane and sickness. Messrs Sensitive and Testy therefore resolve to meet weekly to fill up their "Chest of Groans" with personal experiences of the most horrible kind.

And so they do, accumulating, sigh by sigh, moan by moan, a vast catalogue of tiny Miseries, sauced with apt literary quotations, sprinkled with dreadful puns, and peppered with small explosions of venom and frustration. From time to time Mrs Testy appears to give a feminine viewpoint in "Supplementary Sighs". While Mr Sensitive tends more to the metaphysical Miseries, Mr Testy perpetually urges him to turn his attention to the physical side of things, begging his friend to "give up the double-refined fancy of always leaving the poor body in the basket".

Later in 1806, an expanded version in two volumes appeared, with additional material on the original *Miseries* and some new

"Groans", including "Watering Places". There also appeared a sequel, which Beresford published under the name of Sir Fretful Murmur: *More Miseries, for the Morbid, the Melancholy and the Irritable*. In 1807, a series of sixteen paintings by John Augustus Atkinson was commissioned to illustrate the various Miseries. This was also published in book form, and was followed by a novel called *An Antidote to the Miseries of Human Life*. *Miseries* was also translated into German and French.

In adapting the work for this present edition, we have included parts of the first two books, but omitted most of the personal commentary, quotations and expostulations of Messrs Testy and Sensitive. This is so as not to dilute the Miseries themselves: for it is the grace and wit of the language, incongruously framing the vulgar and comical situations described, which is the great success of the original book, and the part that will prove most ticklish to the humour of modern readers.

But why publish a book about Miseries at all? From the Introduction or *Memoir* to the second book, dated 1st November 1806, comes this explanation from Beresford himself:

7

> *Nature having made me one of those gossamer, sensitive beings upon whom the breath of Heaven cannot blow without creating more or less agitation, I amused myself last year with keeping a Diary of Vexations ... I moreover found that to describe these teasing troubles was to disarm them of their sting, and that one might as quietly contemplate them afterwards as a fine lady might a mouse in a cage, until she wondered that so diminutive an animal could have annoyed her, and resolved that the scratching and midnight ramblings of its kindred should alarm her no more in future.*
>
> *If, however, my irritable reader derives the same comfort from the perusal of my Supplemental Miseries, as I have done from The Miseries of Human Life, then will these sheets be like flowers in a sick chamber that inhale the unwholesome air and breathe it out again with refreshing purity.*

Miseries Personal, Existential and of the Body

What, my poor sir, are the senses, but five yawning inlets to hourly and momentary molestations?
Samuel Sensitive

A villainous cold in the head; blowing your nose lustily and frequently, till you are an abomination to all around you — but without any fruits, except a sharp twinging sensation in the nostrils, as the passage that you have forced open closes up again, with a shrill, thin, whining whistle — not to mention the necessity of disgusting yourself and friends by pronouncing *M* like *B* and *N* like *D*, till you are well.

Being on the bri ... on the bri ... on the bri ... (sneezes) ... ink of a sneeze for a quarter of an hour together; and yet, with all your gasping and sobbing, never able to compass it.

The state of your mouth winding up to a tremendous cold — your lips being metamorphosed into two boiling barrels, totally disqualified for the functions of eating, speaking, laughing, yawning, whistling — and kissing. And the ignominious manner in which your mouth acquits itself of an attempt to speak, or to eat, when its whole interior is parched up by thirst, rage, or fever.

A nervous man upon going to visit a surgeon, being shown into his anatomical museum, including his most notorious failures upon the human species.

Gulping and straining at a pill about the size of a nut; which at last, however, you succeed in getting down to the middle of your throat, where it settles to stay, forever.

Waiting for the operation of an emetic.

When over-fatigued, those self-invited starts, jerks, or twitches that fly about the limbs and body, and come on with an indescribable kind of tingling, teasing, gnawing restlessness; more especially towards bedtime.

The sensation, from the hip downward, when your foot is fast asleep, and before the sharp shooting, which you must now endure, has yet come on.

Suddenly and violently scratching your ear, without recollecting to respect the feelings of an excruciating pimple, with which it is infested.

10 Bending back the fingernail — or even thinking of it. The ends of your fingernails becoming rough and ragged, so as to catch, and pull away, the threads of all your garments.

Groping and stirring with a needle after a thorn in your finger, in the hopes of wheedling out the peeping black atom.

The interval between the dentist's confession that your tooth will be very difficult to draw, and the commencement of the attempt.

A tooth drawn by *instalments*.

Being discriminated from the rest of the human species by so grotesque and distorted a smile that, on producing it before strangers, you must frequently put up with their humane condolences on the spasmodic tortures, under which you seem to be suffering.

All your acquaintances telling you that a portrait, *which you are aware is rather flattering*, is not at all like you. Or, sitting for your portrait to a subordinate painter who renders the likeness with such exasperating exactness, that every wrinkle, blotch and blemish in the face is faithfully represented.

When afflicted with the malady of blushing, to read in the complacent smile of a member of the opposite sex, who has accosted you, that he or she thinks you interested in their attentions.

11

The face or the hands suddenly and unaccountably begrimed by a mysterious sort of filth.

Being obliged to press very hard a very damp or — what is called — a puggy hand.

The sudden deaths that occasionally happen among your family of fingers, in a hard frost.

Explaining to your servant, who is anything but a mechanic, how easy it is to set a steel rat-trap, and just as you have said to him, "There, now, you see the least thing in the world will set it off!", you prove to him the truth of the assertion, by its unexpectedly embracing your own fingers.

After bathing — the dull, rumbling, rushing sound, which continues all day long in your ears, and which all your tweaking, nuzzling and rummaging at them serves only to increase.

The feeling that things are going, just as they have always gone, downwards, backwards, crookedly, spirally, anyhow but upwards, or straightforwards. Or, the knowledge that the stream of your life presents a languid, yet a fretting current, with just enough of agitation to collect a perpetual sediment, which it has not, afterwards, the strength to precipitate or disperse.

The horror of contriving how to adjust one's legs and arms at the age of nineteen in a drawing room.

Getting the Caledonian Cremona when you are just upon the point of marriage.

Catching a violent influenza in the first quartering of the honeymoon.

Hastily marrying a lady, and afterwards discovering that she has an unroselike breath, and her teeth are *not* aromatic pearl.

Having just composed yourself to take a nap on your sofa, eternally tormented by two flies, whom you cannot catch, and who judiciously prefer alighting and washing their hands and faces on your nose and forehead, to regaling on an adjoining saucer full of sweet poison.

After long reclining, with every limb disposed in some peculiarly luxurious manner, to be suddenly routed from your sofa! Then, endeavouring in vain to re-establish yourself in your former posture, of which you have forgotten the particulars, though you recollect the enjoyments, every new attempt leaving a certain void in your comfort, which nothing can supply.

A man whom you have only seen twice, and know nothing of, but who perspires very much in the head, borrowing your pocket comb.

Being seized with a violent bowel complaint whilst you are riding on horseback with two young ladies, to one of whom you are paying your addresses, being obliged to alight in great confusion, telling your fair companions that there is an exquisite bit of scenery round a hedge, which they have just passed, and which you should very much like to sketch, assuring them that you will return in five minutes, and remembering afterwards that it is well known that you never drew in your life.

13

Being shaved on the Cornish coast, in the pilchard season, by the local barber, who embraces your nose with a thumb and finger stinking of said fish.

A pair of pantaloons so constructed with regard to what tailors call the stride, as to limit you to three or four inches per step. In these streights, having to keep pace in walking with a tall friend.

Miseries of the Table

Shall I have the pleasure of sending you a little more?

*"The **pleasures** of the table!" — yes — a sly ironical rogue was he that first hit upon that expression. I fancy my dog Rover would give us a much better account of the pleasures under the table ...*
Timothy Testy

Slipping your knife suddenly and violently from off a bone, its edge first shrieking across the plate (so as to make you hated by yourself and the whole company), and then driving the plate before it, and lodging all its contents — meat, gravy, melted butter, vegetables, &c., &c., partly on your own breeches, partly on the cloth, partly on the floor, but principally on the lap of a charming girl who sits by you, and to whom you had been diligently endeavouring to recommend yourself as a suitor.

After forwardly offering your services in cutting up a fine, greasy goose, or a ham, with a very short-bladed knife, lubricating your thumb and third finger with the fat at every incision, not to mention the almost inseparability of the odour, which in consequence perfumes every part of your body and the cuff of your coat. Moreover, in the execution of this oily duty, being obliged to make a practical confession, before twenty watchful witnesses, that you have no genius for carving.

15

Attempting to cut and serve cauliflower or asparagus with a spoon; the fate of the cargo (which you had neglected to insure), is well known: ditto as to jelly, which instantly bids adieu to the spoon, and quivers like quicksilver about the cloth.

The spinning plate: there is but one, and you always have it.

The moment in which you discover that you have taken a mouthful of fat, by mistake for a turnip.

Finding a human hair in your mouth, which, as you slowly draw it forth, seems to lengthen, ad infinitum.

Grinding upon tough, sinewy meat with supposititious teeth.

Biting a piece of cheek almost out, and then perpetually catching it between your teeth during the remainder of your meal, and for a fortnight afterwards.

Long after you have finished your own temperate meal, seeing the sixth or seventh plate of turtle, venison, &c., conveyed into a Living Larder immediately opposite you.

After eating mushrooms, the lively interest you take in the debate that accidentally follows upon the question whether they were of the right sort. Or, suddenly discovering by the palate, instead of the nose, that you have let in a bad oyster!

16

Using nut-crackers, which, in the act of refusing to seize the shell for you with their teeth, contrive, nevertheless, to bite your finger with their legs.

The long and painful apprenticeship that you serve to the business of learning to like olives — without being master of your trade at last.

On meeting with some long-forgotten bon-bon of your childhood (treacle, liquorice, periwinkles, &c.), and snapping it up with a sort of sentimental voracity, and instantly and violently rejecting it, in a paroxysm of nausea.

Triumphantly producing from your cellar the last remaining bottle of some choice old wine, previously announced to your friends as the boast of the bin, but which, when decanted, shows a desperately cloudy aspect. Or, on opening several hampers of precious wine — just arrived from a great distance — finding that the bottles have almost all bled to death, in consequence of quarrelling and fighting along the way.

Vainly attempting, when in great haste, to make a very hard lump of sugar melt by pushing and pressing it against the side of the tumbler — to no effect but that of slipping off the spoon with a jerk, and splashing the hot liquor up into your own eyes.

Coffee brought in a cup without a saucer — the cup so full that the slightest motion of the spoon spills the hot staining liquor on your new trousers (cream is out of the question, as the cup was at first too full to hold another drop). To crown it all, you must appear to be quite easy in mind and body.

17

The handle of a *full* tea-cup coming off in your hand, just as you are raising it to your mouth.

On coming down late to a hasty breakfast, finding the last drop of water in your kettle boiling away, the toast in ashes, and the cat just finishing your cream.

In the depths of Winter, trying in vain to effect a union between unsoftened butter and the crumb of a very stale loaf, or a quite new one.

Wishing to have an early breakfast, and the kettle refusing, as if by fatality, to boil.

The top of your tea-pot suddenly slipping off while you are cautiously dribbling its scanty contents into your cup. Or, a tea-pot that won't pour except through the top — that which you intend for your cup trickling instead down your fingers, into your sleeve and over the cloth.

Letting fall (of course on the buttered side), the piece of roll, or muffin, on which you had set your heart.

Weak, bad, cold, cloudy coffee, with poor milk — and but little of that. Likewise, tea made with smoke, as well as water.

18

Trying to harpoon a floating pat of butter.

At breakfast, honey dripping through the apertures of your bread, and over the sides, upon your fingers. Or, cutting bread and butter with a knife, the handle of which has been touched by someone whose fingers have come in contact with honey. Then, being hurried away, without a moment allowed for washing your hands: or — since that cannot possibly be granted you — chopping them off.

I think I will trouble you again, it is really so — very — thank you —

Your sensations about the throat and chest, after having too hastily forced down a piece of very hard, dry biscuit. Or, eating a biscuit so unguardedly that the crumbs keep showering into your bosom, and you are under the necessity of cherishing them next to your skin for the rest of the day.

The infatuation of mumping your way through a large and very sour apple, though you are soon reduced to your front teeth (grinders *hors de combat* at the first crunch), and would give your life that it were all well over.

While you are swallowing a raspberry, discovering by its taste that you have been so unhappy as to occasion the death of a harmless insect!

Your tongue coming into contact with the skin of a peach — or even the mind coming into contact with the idea!

After having breakfasted in bed — to which you are confined — rolling, through the rest of the day and night, in crumbs, which are presently baked by your body into innumerable needles of crust.

19

In rushing out to dinner, clean and smart, becoming hot with your exercise, the consciousness of which makes you still hotter; so that, on arriving, too late to repair yourself, you are obliged to sit down to table with a large party (each of whom is clean and fresh), with plastered hair and a red, varnished face.

Taking a walk in the garden of a friend with whom you are engaged to dine, unexpectedly passing by the kitchen, and seeing the cookmaid chewing the parsley previous to mixing it with the butter for the fowls that you are to have for dinner, by which process she saves herself the very unnecessary trouble of boiling and chopping it.

The soup is delicious!

not any more I thank you.

Dropping in upon a friend at dinner time, on the strength of a general invitation, and at once discovering, from the countenance and manner of his wife, that you'd better have waited for a particular one.

Dining at a house where your bountiful hostess spares you all the trouble of determining for yourself what quantity of food your health and inclination require — where, if you venture but to turn your head, you are sure of finding that another pound of provisions has been dexterously juggled on your plate, during the momentary absence of your eyes.

A public dinner in June — with the opening recommendation that you are to partake it with a snug party of five or six hundred perfect strangers, all to be served by about the proportion of one waiter to fifty feeders.

On arriving at the said dinner, finding your nameplate removed from your rightful table. After a fruitless squabble with your sturdy substitute, you at length proceed in procuring a seat at an extempore, castaway table, by the ever-opening door; your seat in a cramped corner, where you wind and screw yourself in, and there sit, squeezed like a cheese in a press, on a bare, narrow, shelving bench, far, far away from all your friends, your new set being nothing more than savages.

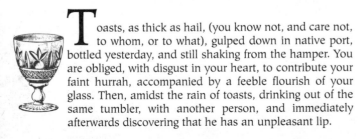

Toasts, as thick as hail, (you know not, and care not, to whom, or to what), gulped down in native port, bottled yesterday, and still shaking from the hamper. You are obliged, with disgust in your heart, to contribute your faint hurrah, accompanied by a feeble flourish of your glass. Then, amidst the rain of toasts, drinking out of the same tumbler, with another person, and immediately afterwards discovering that he has an unpleasant lip.

Miseries Domestic *including the* Dressing Room *and* Bed-Chamber

What is your house, while you are in it, but a prison filled with nests of little reptiles — of insect-annoyances — which torment you more because they cannot kill you? What are the familiar operations of dressing and undressing, but stinging remembrances of the privileged nakedness of the Savage?
Samuel Sensitive

Losing the keys to all your most private repositories; by which you suffer a double embarrassment — that you cannot, yourself, get at what you want; and that they have, probably, fallen into the hands of others, who both can, and will.

Vainly hunting, a thousand times over, in every corner, nook and cranny of the house, for something you have lost, till, at some future period, when you have long abandoned the pursuit, the truant article appears of its own accord.

22 Grinding dirt into the carpet, in turning upon your heel; then, after stooping, in a frenzy, to pick up the filthy fragments, and at last walking away satisfied that you have done so, crushing fresh parcels of dirt in other parts and so on for an hour.

Dropping something, when you are either too lame, or too lazy, to get up for it; and almost breaking your ribs, and quite throwing yourself down, by stretching down to it over the arm of your chair, without, at last, reaching it.

Toiling at a rotten cork with a broken screw, and so dragging it out piecemeal — except the fragments, which drop in the bottle.

Squatting plump on an unsuspected cat in your chair.

Bottling of home-made wines — and all the stooping, cork-haggling, finger-freezing, rim-hammering, bottle-breaking, stock-slopping, nose-poisoning, &c., which you have to go through for a whole morning together.

Scissors that pinch, instead of cutting.

Feeling your arm and elbow cold and — on looking farther into the matter — perceiving that you have long been leaning in slop, which has dabbled you to the skin.

A cupboard in the parlour in which you are making love — with the consequent perpetual intrusion of one prying servant after another, clattering among the shelves with glasses, tea-things, &c. — and all this, just towards the crisis of reciprocal confessions!

In attempting to take up the poker softly (an invalid asleep in the room), dropping it violently down, sociably accompanied by the tongs and shovel in its fall.

Cleansing the Augean stables; or, in other words, undertaking the labour of digesting into its proper place each of a thousand different articles, of as many different uses, sorts and sizes (books, phials, papers, fiddles, mathematical instruments, drawings and knick-knacks without end), which have been for weeks or months accumulating.

The interval between breaking a pane of glass and the arrival of the glazier. (N.B. the aspect of your apartment being East–North-East, the wind setting in full from that quarter, the glazier a drunkard, living seven miles off.)

After having sent for a remarkably clever carpenter for the purpose of doing a variety of jobs that require both a nice hand and a contriving head — seeing enter, in his stead, a drivelling dormouse, who just knows a hammer from a nail.

23

The machinery of the window-sash rudely and furiously slapping down, without a moment's warning, with the force (if not the effect), of a guillotine.

In lathering the face, before shaving, very early in the morning, while still half-asleep, yawning so suddenly as to slap the full brush into your mouth.

Shaving after a frosty walk (when the face is pimpled, skin tender and hand tremulous), with cold water, hard brush, ropy soap, and a blunt razor. Then, at the first onset, saluting your chin with a deep gash so that, through the remainder of the operation, your face and fingers are dabbled in blood, which enrages you by flowing faster than you can wash it away.

24

Pushing up your shirtsleeves for the purpose of washing your hands — but so ineffectually that, in the midst of the operation, they fall and bag down over your wet, soapy wrists.

After washing your hands in icy water, dangling them before you like a dancing bear, while you ferret about in vain for a towel.

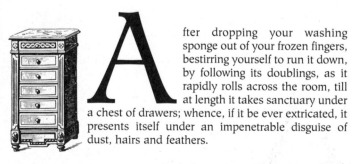

After dropping your washing sponge out of your frozen fingers, bestirring yourself to run it down, by following its doublings, as it rapidly rolls across the room, till at length it takes sanctuary under a chest of drawers; whence, if it be ever extricated, it presents itself under an impenetrable disguise of dust, hairs and feathers.

Having forgotten to lay in a fresh supply of toothbrushes, battering your teeth with the handle, and pricking your gums with the bristles of your old one, completely grubbed out in the middle — its few remaining hairs staring off horizontally on all sides. Then, the moment in which a misgiving comes over you, that *someone else* has clandestinely assisted you in wearing out your toothbrush.

The feelings of your teeth and gums, when you have insulted them by an over-proportion of strong toothpaste.

Tying your neck-tie vilely, when you wish to be particularly seducing. Or, dressing for a ball by an ill-cast looking-glass, and so mourning and wondering over your own unseasonable ugliness.

25

After having lost your sleeve-button, without knowing it, rashly thrusting your hand into the arm of your coat, and so carrying the shirtsleeve in a bunch up to the shoulder

Getting out of bed in the morning, after having had far too much sleep. Or, after tossing through a restless night, at last slinking into a doze, from which you instantly start broad awake, with the joy of thinking that you are falling asleep.

The two-fold torment inflicted by a flea: first, the persecution to which he subjects you through the night; second, the loss of your meditated revenge in the morning, by his hocus-pocus escapes — his unthought-of and incredible capers, leaps and flings from under your eager fingers, at the very instant when you seem in the act of ... nay, to have *actually* annihilated him.

Loudly bursting three or four buttons of your tight waistcoat, the fastenings of your braces and the strings of your pantaloons behind, in fetching a deep sigh — dead silence in the company, at the moment of the melancholy explosion.

A clock posted within a yard of your pillow, which, besides confidentially clicking every second in your ear, as long as your eyes are open, regularly wakes you with mentioning the hour.

Sleeping aslant, or lying in a bed so made that you feel yourself all night long going down a hill, with a precipice at the end of it.

26 Waking up with the pain of finding that you are doing your best to bite your own tongue off.

The sheet untracked, or too short, so as to bring the legs into close unwanted intimacy with the loathsome, coarse hairs of the blanket.

Being serenaded at your window, all night long, by the tender war-whoop of two cats, performed with demoniacal variations and professional enthusiasm.

In attempting to untie the strings of your drawers, at going to bed very sleepy, dragging them into a cluster of hard knots — with your subsequent frenzy from nipping and picking at them for an hour till your nails are sore; no knife.

Suddenly recollecting, as you lie upstairs in bed at a very late hour of a Lapland night, that you have neglected to see that the fires are all safe below; then, after an agonizing interval of hesitation, crawling out like a culprit, and quivering downstairs.

Miseries of Travelling

What are carriages, but cages upon wheels? What are riding-horses, but purchased enemies, whom you pamper into strength, as well as inclination, to kick your brains out?
Samuel Sensitive

In riding against the wind, feeling a great insect dash into your eye — then, after carrying it home in agony, and sitting for an hour while the socket is rummaged with the corner of a handkerchief, your eye left sorer than ever, the animal seeming considerably grown, since he first took shelter under your penthouse lid.

In travelling through an uninhabited country, enquiring your way of different Rustics, each of whom, besides giving you unintelligible directions as to your road, represents the place in question as many miles further off than it had been reported by the last ... together with their rigmarole wonderings and lamentations at the number of miles that you have travelled out of your way.

Or, having lost your way, being in great haste, and asking a stuttering family to direct you to the place of your destination.

28

In speeding through towns and turnpikes, the nervous halts and desperate manoeuvres to which you are perpetually driven, to avoid gratifying successive shoals of children, in their eager wishes and strenuous endeavours to be run over.

Sleeping, on a sudden and desperate emergency, at a low lodging-house — your head broken, at the outset, by the beam of your chamber door. Then, for the interior — floor all hill and dale, no fireplace, one crazy chair, a litter of sleepless brats hard by, with only a half-inch panel between *their* throats and *your* ears, knotty mattress, no soap, only rainwater and *that* but a spoonful in a wine bottle, all black at the bottom, but one towel, or rather duster, about six inches wide, counting in the holes, cat left under your bed, and kittening over you in the night.

Or, in the room of an inn to which you are confined by rain, examining the scrawled window-panes, in the hopes of curious verses, and finding nothing more *piquant* than: "I love pretty Sally Appleby of Chipping-Norton"; "I am very unhappy — Sam Jennings"; or "Wm Wilkins is a fool", with "So are you" written underneath...Then, for your evening recreations: after having for the twentieth time, held a candle to the wretched prints, or ornaments with which the room is hung, such as female personifications of the Four Seasons, or the Cardinal Virtues, daubed with purple, red and raspberry-cream colour, or a series of halfpenny prints called "Going out in the Morning", "Starting a Hare", "Coming in at the Death", &c., or a Jemmy Jessamy lover in a wood, in new boots, but without purse, whip, horse or hat, with hair full dressed, on one knee, in the dirt, before a coy May-pole Miss in an old-fashioned riding dress; both figures being partly coloured and partly plain; or, a pair of maps of England, with only about four counties, and no towns in them, worked in two samplers by the landlady's twin daughter, "aged ten years", or, a little fat plaster-man on the chimney piece with his gilt cocked hat at the back of his head ...

29

At the same inn, asking, in despair, for some books, which, when brought, turn out to be: *Bracken's Farriery*; three or four wrecks of different spelling books; *Gauging Made Easy*; a few odd volumes of the *Racing Calendar*; and an abridged abridgement of the *History of England* in question and answer, with half the leaves torn out and the other half illegible with greasy thumbing. In each, you try a few pages, nod over them till nine o'clock, and then stumble to bed in a cloud of disgust.

On opening your trunk, after a long journey, discovering that the perfume contained in an ill-packed canister has burst its cearments and grimed itself into your clean linen, &c.

O n entering a stagecoach for a long journey, finding (amongst other unpleasant inmates), at least one muddling mother, with a sick — but not silent — infant: windows all as close as wax, for the *poor child's* sake!

J ust as you are going off — with only one other person on your side of the coach, who, you flatter yourself, is the last — seeing the door suddenly opened, and the guard craning, shoving, and buttressing up an overgrown, puffing, greasy, human Hog, of the butcher or grazier-breed — the whole machine straining and groaning under its cargo. By dint of incredible efforts and contrivances, the Carcase is, at length, weighed up to the door. And when, at length, the whole Beast is fairly slung in, plunged down and bedded, with the squelch of a falling Ox and the grunt of a Rhinoceros, you find yourself suddenly viced in, from the shoulder to the hip; upon which the Monster begins to make himself merry with your misery, and keeps braying away, totally callous to the dumb frowns or muttered execrations of the whole coach.

30

T ravelling in a mail-coach one hundred and eighty miles, and all the way having your nose offended by the most horrible stench, which each of the passengers thinks proceeds from his neighbour, and upon arriving at the Swan with Two Necks, discovering that the *mauvaise odeur* issued from a putrid hare under one of the seats, which, owing to the carelessness of the guard, has been permitted to perform two journeys to town.

S eeing, at the door of an inn at which the coach stops, a most bewitching creature, with whom you fall, instantly, deeply and inextricably in love — but who suddenly trips away, and is succeeded at her post by a Harridan, with a face tattooed with wrinkles — the very home of ugliness and spite; and who continues as the substitute of your charmer during the remainder of your halt.

While passing in the mail-coach through a delightful country, catching perpetual glimpses of the most picturesque scenes, or objects, from which, however, you are unfeelingly whirled away.

The attempts at sleep that you make in a night-coach, under the following lulling circumstances: no night-cap, clapping your head against the side panel from which it is incessantly cuffed and bumped away by the jumps and jolts of the coach, your knees miserably cramped, your opposite neighbour continually bobbing forward in his sleep into your stomach. Then, just as you are, at last, sinking into something very like a nap, making a dead stop at the inn where the passengers are to sup; when you all yawn, limp, shiver and blunder along, in the dark, to a cold room, where you sit in gloomy, weary, numb, stupid silence, waiting without end for the supper, which, when brought in at last, you cannot touch, though very hungry; till, at length, you crawl, jaded and grumbling, back to your endless, hopeless, harassing journey. On looking out the window at daybreak, you find that you are just taking leave of a sublime or beautiful country, through which you have been stealing all night; and entering on a dull, barren, flat landscape, which continues through the day — as it had done through the day before.

31

On stopping at a public house, in the middle of a burning day, eagerly ordering something to drink, which the waiting is so long in bringing that the coachman will wait no longer; then, the moment when he has driven off, looking wistfully back, and seeing a fine frothy tankard brought out for you; the coachman inexorable.

fter you have rashly ventured upon an unexamined sandwich at an inn, discovering, as you get on, that it contains more butter (and that bad) than bread; and, for one inch of lean, four or five of stringy fat.

After starting on a very long journey, through a variety of strange counties, discovering that you have left your travel guide behind, so that you see everything in profound ignorance; not knowing whether the town through which you are passing is Kidderminster or Aberdeen — the other passengers all being fools, or foreigners, with no light to throw on the difficulty.

On opening a book entitled *A Faithful Guide to ... and its Environs*, finding that it should have been: *A Hotchpotch of Misinformation, chiefly Stolen, and Spoiled in Stealing*.

32

On looking down from the top of a steeple, precipice, &c., taking its altitude by means of the sudden dizziness that seizes you, accompanied with that sinking, thrilling, tingling qualm, which darts from your heart to your ankles, as you shrink backward from your perpendicular peep.

On your return from an excursion to North Wales, the Lakes, &c., being asked by the first friend you meet whether you saw X, the most celebrated spot of the whole tour — the only place, however, by some villainous mischance, you did *not* see.

A tour on the Continent, or in other words, a long fit of sea-sickness, introductory to a series of journeys, presenting: carriages without springs, horses without strength, postillions without feeling, cookery without cleanliness, beds not without vermin, charges without moderation, houses without friends, questions without answers, absence without letters, and Miseries without end.

Miseries of Social Life

Thorns, pins, needles (and, I would add, tongues) are always in the way, and always pointed; nor is there ever wanting some industrious body at your elbow who is, at all times, in cheerful readiness to stick them.

Samuel Sensitive

Diffidently entering a full room, every chair occupied, and no one standing to keep you company.

Sitting down alone in a large party upon a sofa that makes an *equivocal* noise.

After having left a company in which you have been galled by the raillery of some wag, thinking, at your leisure, of a repartee, which, if it had been discharged at the proper moment, would have blown him to atoms.

34

Suddenly thinking of your best argument in a debate, and, in your eagerness to state it, swallowing your wine the wrong way, and so squeaking and croaking more and more unintelligibly, with the tears running down your cheeks.

Preparing a company to laugh at a good story, and finding that not a risible muscle moves.

Finding yourself reduced by your own stupidity either to beg for an explanation of a joke that all the rest of the company are enjoying, or to keep your gravity, while you are longing to lose it.

After telling, at much length, a scarce and curious anecdote, with considerable marks of self-complacency at having it to tell, being quietly reminded by the person you have been so kindly instructing, that you had heard it first — *from himself!*

After having related to a company, a piece of intelligence you thought was known only to yourself, finding that they had been talking about it half an hour previous to your entrance, though they were too polite to interrupt you in relation to it.

After a long and animated debate with a friend, in the dark, and just as you have drawn forth all your strongest arguments, and are beginning exultingly to infer from his long silence that you have completely worsted him, and that he has not another word to say — receiving his answer in a strong, steady snore, which shows him to have been in a sweet sleep for the last quarter of an hour.

Sitting opposite a man who squints, and answering him when he is addressing another person.

In a very polite circle — the convulsive and portentous termination of your well-modulated titter in an involuntary short snort.

Being compelled by a deaf person, in a large and silent company, to repeat some very inane remark three or four times over, at the highest pitch of your voice.

Endeavouring to laugh with your companions at an incident that still gives you excruciating pain.

Having been promised a present by a friend (which he never sent), discovering, from some indirect remarks of his, that *he thinks he has.*

To be obliged frequently to meet in company a man who opposes every remark for the purpose of starting an argument, in which he is always more vociferous than convincing.

Grating the sensibility, the prepossessions, the self-love, the vanity, &c., of the person to whom you are speaking, by some unguarded words, which, as soon as you have uttered them, you would die to eat; then, floundering and plunging, deeper and deeper, in your wild and confused attempts to recover yourself.

When in a nervous and irritable mood, sitting with one who has an unceasing trick of swinging himself in his chair like a pendulum — working his foot up and down like a knife-grinder — beating his nails or knuckles like a drummer's, &c., &c.

After a long pause in conversation with a near stranger, re-addressing him at the same instant as he re-addresses you: a polite and dead stop on both sides. Then, after a reasonable time mutually given and taken for resuming the stifled speech, without effect — both chancing, at the same point of time, to venture again.

To be seized with morbid and irresistible sleepiness, while in conversation with persons who have every title to your respect.

After dinner, with a favourite party, when the cloth has been removed, and the wine of the conversation, as well as of the bottle, is just beginning to brighten — seeing the door open, and a string of staring babies brought in, and carried round, to be caressed and admired, during the rest of the sitting. Then, after the first or prelusive squall of a fractious brat — which you had taken into your arms, to please its mother — the horrible pause during which you perceive that it is collecting breath to burst to with a fresh and recruited scream that is to thrill through your marrow.

At table, after dinner, hearing one of your children's little, but loud, impromptus upon the pimples luxuriantly budding out upon the nose of one of your visitors.

The state of writhing torture into which you are occasionally thrown by the sudden and unexpected questions, or remarks, of a child, before a large company; a little wretch of your own, for instance, who will run up to an unmarried lady and then harrow you by crying out, before you have time to gag it, "Now do, miss, let me count the creases in your face — there's one, there's two, there's three," and so on, or, accosting another lady in the same explicit strain, electrifies you by breaking out with, "Why do you come here so often? For, do you know, my Aunt always says she can't abide you — don't you, Aunt?"

The miscarriage of a letter announcing the day and hour of your visit to a friend; so that, on your arrival on horseback, after a long journey late at night, you find the family all abed. When, after an hour's bawling and knocking, you have succeeded in bringing a servant to the window, and, with great difficulty, convinced him that you are not a mad house-breaker, you are, at length, let in, and, on exploring the deserted rooms, in search of warmth and refreshment, find no better entertainment than fires raked out, an empty larder, the cellar locked up, no bed prepared, &c., &c.

37

Sleeping in a dark room, in a dark night, in a strange house, and, after being kept awake by the most mysterious sounds for three hours, at length beginning to be satisfied that they proceed from an unusually active mouse.

Invading a humble, regular family (while quietly assembled round the dinner table), upon the wrong day. On entering the room, you catch the footman in the act of removing the cloth — now to be re-laid, and slowly spread with the lukewarm ruins of the late meal, tumultuously remanded from the kitchen, half-rescued as it is from the clutches of the Hogs and Harpies below, and alternately seasoned, as you proceed, with stigmas upon every fork-full you take up, and panegyrics upon the delightful party with whom you were anxiously expected to partake it *on the day before.*

Being followed by your terrier into a drawing room and before you can stop him, seeing him kill the tortoiseshell cat belonging to the lady of the house, who, notwithstanding every explanation, persists in thinking that you brought the dog for that express purpose.

Paying a long visit to the house of a well-meaning, retired soul, whose only idea of entertaining you is that of never leaving you a moment by yourself.

Living with, or even visiting, one whose feelings differ widely from your own with regard to the admission of fresh air.

38 **D**elaying to return a dull visit so long that, when you return it at last, it is rendered doubly formidable by the cold and stiff reception that you expect, and find; to say nothing of the torments to which you have condemned yourself by keeping suspended over your head the evil hour, which you knew all along must come upon you in the end; and that, in truth, you have been continually paying the dreaded visit for whole weeks together.

Sitting on with a *sepulchral* party after supper, two or three hours beyond the time at which you had ordered your carriage, but with which your drunken coachman is unable to come, so that you, at last, walk home five or six miles in the rain.

On an afternoon visit in the country — receiving a summons to attend a few *Cats* (who think themselves *Kittens*), in their evening promenade; meanwhile, the enchanting girl who formed your sole attraction to the house is confined at home by a slight indisposition, which would only have rendered her additionally interesting.

Falling into a party who have lived so much together as to have a thousand topics, jests, allusions, &c., in common, which are perpetually bandied from eye to eye, and from mouth to mouth — you quite abroad the whole time, and sitting like a foreigner among natives. Or, falling among a junto of lawyers, or physicians, or merchants, or naval captains, &c. — all, except yourself, of one profession — who instantly and hotly begin to discuss the driest and most technical points relating to their cause.

Being prevailed upon by your friend to accompany him to a dinner party to which you have *not* been invited, and upon your introduction to the lady of the house, she expressses her regret that her dining room is so *small*, and immediately afterwards obliquely observes with a freezing *but*, that she can manage very well, as her *brother* can sit at a side-table.

Knocking at a door, and, by a horrible and unaccountable lapse of memory, forgetting the name of the master or mistress of the house.

39

On entering the room, to join an evening party composed of remarkably grave, strict and precise persons, suddenly to find out that you are drunk, and (what is still worse), that the company has shared with you in the discovery.

At a dinner table — being placed at the bottom, while all the choicest and liveliest people are thrown to the top — you longing to be among them, and to join their flights of fancy, instead of grinding along, with your neighbours at the drowsy end of the table, in their broad-wheeled wagons, on the milestone of matter-of-fact.

Falling in with a fellow who thinks he can entertain you by reciting in detail the dishes, courses and cookery of his favourite dinners for the last month.

A person who treats you in all respects (the fee excepted), like his doctor, unreservedly laying before you, while he is helping you to dinner, all the minutest particulars of his most revolting ailments.

Obliged, out of politeness, to caress your hostess's favourite lap-dog, which has sore eyes and bad breath.

After a flat evening visit — long after you have been tortured with violent longings to be gone — endeavouring, at last, to catch the eye of your tattling wife and interchange the mysterious signal; yet, though you have pointed her like a partridge for an hour, she will *not rise*.

40 At breakfast — hearing a boring person detail, at full length, their last night's long, dull dream ... and then the interpretation of it, in all its parts!

Being invited to a wedding dinner when you have just discovered the inconstancy of your wife.

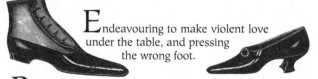

Endeavouring to make violent love under the table, and pressing the wrong foot.

Being caught in the act of ogling the object of your desire by the tattling She-Tabby from whom you are most desirous of concealing your tender anguish.

Meeting a young lady for the first time after an intended match is broken off (love tolerably, but not excessively deep), looking like two shy cats, each obliquely watching the other to see what degree of dejection the separation has produced.

At a dance, pointing out to your beautiful partner, the ludicrous vulgarity of a man who, she blushingly informs you, is her brother.

Hearing the bells ring for the marriage of your rival.

Being called in as an umpire in a matrimonial quarrel, which leaves you the choice of being shipwrecked on one of the following six rocks:

- *That of remaining silent* (for which both parties hate you; each supposing that you secretly favour the other)

41

- *That of pronouncing that both are in the wrong* (for which you are, obviously, hated by both)

- *That of insinuating that both may be in the right* (hatred, again, on both sides)

- *That of defending the lady at the expense of the gentleman* (still hated by both; by her, for attacking her *caro sposo*, whom she will suffer no one to despise but herself; by him, for siding with the enemy)

- *That of defending the gentleman at the expense of the lady* (this case is, inversely, the same as the last)

- *That of endeavouring to make peace by treating the matter lightly* (for which both are far too much in earnest, as well as far too eager for victory, not to hate *you* most of all)

The best course, perhaps, if you cannot steal away, is to be taken with a sudden and violent fit of toothache, which may last *ad libitum*.

Miseries of the Country, including Country Walks and Gardens

42

What is the country, but a sandy desert at one season, or a swallowing quagmire at another?
Samuel Sensitive

The Miseries of country walks: stooping, tearing, floundering and bleeding your way through a muddy, briary copse, with here and there a rushy pool, which takes you by surprise, so that you are more and more entangled and engulfed as you advance, till you are, after all, obliged to turn back and repeat all your sufferings; and so emerge at last, looking like a half-murdered beggar.

The sole of your shoe torn down in walking, and obliging you to lift your foot and limp along, like a pig on a string. Meanwhile, your boot is continually taking in gravel; while, for a time, you try to calm your feelings by believing it to be only hard dirt, and vainly hoping that it will presently relieve you by pulverizing. And, with the heel of one muddy shoe, treading the loosened string out of the other; corns on every toe.

Suddenly rousing yourself from the ennui of a solitary walk by striking your toe (with a blister at the end of it), full and hard against the sharp corner of a fixed stone.

When you have trusted your foot on a frozen rut — the ice proving treacherous, and bedding you in slush, to the hip. And, in falling, laying hold of the ankle of a lady with whom you are walking (said lady somewhat stricken in years), and drawing her after you.

Feeling your foot slidder over the back of a toad, which you took for a stepping-stone, in your dark, evening walk. In the like manner, crushing snails, beetles, slugs, &c., whether you wish to do so or not.

In your evening walk, being closely followed, for a quarter of an hour, by a large bulldog (without his master), who keeps up a stifled growl, with his muzzle nuzzling about your calf, or thighs, as if choosing out the fleshiest bite.

While you are out with a walking-party (after heavy rains), one shoe suddenly sucked off by the boggy clay; and then, in making a long and desperate stretch (which fails), with the hope of recovering it, the *other* left in the same predicament: the second stage of ruin is that of standing, or rather tottering, in blank despair, with both feet bare, planted, ankle-deep in the quagmire. The last (I had almost said the dying) scene of the tragedy — that of deliberately cramming, first one, and then the other, clogged, polluted foot into its choked-up shoe.

44

While walking with others, in a line, through a narrow path, being perpetually addressed by the lady immediately before you, who, although she never turns her head in speaking, and a roaring wind, from behind, flies away with every soft syllable as it is uttered (like an eagle with a dove), seems to consider you as provokingly stupid for making her repeat her words twenty times over.

Just in that period of your walk when you are overtaken by a torrent of rain, and secretly applauding your own caution in having provided yourself with an umbrella, said umbrella is suddenly and furiously reversed by a puff of wind and shredded to ribbons in an instant.

Passing unawares through a paddock inhabited by an old Bull, by no means celebrated for urbanity to strangers.

Jumping in sacks at a country fair and, in the midst of the diversion, hearing that a mad bull is coming down the street.

Seeing a cow skip and frisk, and affect the graces.

After watching, for a while, with reasonable satisfaction, the vagaries of a lot of lambs, to see the little ones break off from their business, whilst all of a sudden, the contagion of quips and cranks, unaccountably and immoderately, seizes upon their shaggy, quaggy dams, who, quite forgetting their years, gravity and incumbrances, begin to lumber and flounder about, heaving themselves at least half an inch into the air, squelching down again, and, in the course of their cumbrous capers and pirouettes, working and walloping their bales of wool and cargoes of suet through the whole conglomerated mass of collops, tripes and blubber, from haunch to throttle. So much for Arcadian delights!

45

Walking in clean, leather breeches down a hill, meeting a flock of sheep, which has been driven twenty miles in a muddy road, one of which, being pursued by the sheep dog, runs between your legs.

While you are laughing, or talking wildly to yourself, in walking, suddenly seeing a person steal close by you, who, you are sure, must have heard it all; then, in an agony of shame, making a wretched attempt to sing, in a voice as like your talk as possible, in the hopes of making your hearer think that you had been only singing all the while.

In returning home from a long, hot ride, being overtaken on a common, many miles from home, by a torrent of rain, which so completely drenches your heated body that you are obliged, for the preservation of your life, to stop at some lone, mean public house, undress and get between the blankets while your clothes are drying. Then, after you have lain awake like a fool for a couple of hours, doing nothing in the busy part of the day, finding, when you have re-dressed yourself, the rain increasing, night coming on, and no messenger to be had.

Residing, at a Country town, next door to a quiet neighbour, whose dwelling is suddenly converted into an alehouse of the most *cheerful* description.

Living, or even making a stay, within close earshot of a ring of execrable bells, execrably rung for some hours every evening.

Being conducted by an enthusiastic agriculturalist round an extensive farm, having no taste whatever for the breeding of sheep, fattening of pigs, new invented draining and threshing machines, &c., &c.

46

After having assembled a dinner party on Michaelmas Day, finding that the *fox* has taken upon himself to execute the orders you had given to the servants with regard to the *goose*.

On an August evening — windows open, and candles lighted — the incessant visits of gnats, moths, earwigs and so on without invitation; so that, one half of your time passes in killing some of your guests, and the other in helping the rest to kill themselves.

While in the act of boasting at your own table that your peas, by much the most forward in the county, will be ready for table in a fortnight at the farthest — to be interrupted in the midst of your exultations by the entrance of a plate of them *actually* ready, and sent into your kitchen that morning, as a present from the rival garden of a neighbour.

Having a suspicion that your neighbours have purloined your turnips, you hang your horse at the gate, while you ascertain the truth of your conjectures, and upon your return you find that your horse has been made away with in your absence.

Miseries of the Town

What are Towns, but an upper Tartarus of smoke and din?
Samuel Sensitive

While you are harmlessly reading, or writing, in a room that fronts the street, being compelled, during the whole morning, to undergo that savage jargon of yells, brays and screams from dustmen, beggars, muffin-mongers, knife-grinders and newscarriers ... but, should you chance to have a wish for what is in the baskets or barrows of these shark-mouthed bawlers, being obliged to let them pass unstopped, from your utter incapability of ever achieving the slightest smattering in any of their infernal dialects, which they have palpably invented for the sole purpose of guarding against the smallest risk of being, by any accident, understood.

Living in chambers under a man who takes private lessons in dancing.

Stopping in the street to address a person whom you know rather too well to pass without speaking, and yet not quite well enough to have a word to say to — *he* feeling himself in the same dilemma, so that, after each has asked, and answered, the question "How do you do?", you stand silently face to face, apropos to nothing, for a minute; and then part in a transport of awkwardness.

Accosting a person in the street with the utmost familiarity, shaking him long and cordially by the hand, and, at length, discovering by his cold (or, if he is a fool, angry) stare, that he is not the man you took him for.

Or, finding that the person with whom you thus claim acquaintance has entirely forgotten you, though you perfectly remember *him*.

On taking shelter from a storm, under a gateway, finding yourself face to face with the very person from whom you had long been concealing, by all possible stratagems, the fact of your being in town.

Walking briskly forwards, while you are looking backwards, and so advancing towards another walker, who is doing the same; then meeting, with the shock of two battering rams, which drives your whole stock of breath out of your body ... At length, after a mutual burst of execrations, you each move, for several minutes, side by side, *with the same motion*, in endeavouring to pass on.

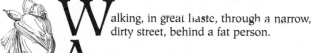

Walking, in great haste, through a narrow, dirty street, behind a fat person.

As you walk forth — freshly and sprucely dressed — receiving in full, at a sharp turning, the filthy flirtings of a well-turned mop.

Passing under a pot-plant garden, which you had not observed, projecting from a window, just at the moment when its rural mistress is watering her half-withered, swarthy sweet peas and myrtles, the mould hard, and the water running over into the street.

49

The manner in which a fish-woman unfolds her opinions of you, when you have unintentionally drawn them forth by overturning her full basket.

As you are walking with your charmer, meeting a drunken beggar, who, as he staggers by you, ejects his reserve of tobacco against the lady's coat... or, worse, being followed by an uncouth sailor and his trull, both talking very noisily and indecently, your endeavours, by a quick step and rapid, loud observations, to prevent the lady from hearing their foul oaths and obscene suggestions.

Crouching and crawling through the scaffolding, ladders, rubbish, flying smother and tumbling bricks of a half-built house — and all this without having made your will.

On returning to your house very late at night, or rather early in the morning, discovering that, in the act of rapping on the door, you are rocking the cradle of an abandoned natural child, very *un*naturally suspended at your knocker.

When you are peaceably reading your paper at a coffee house, two friends, perfect strangers to you, squatting themselves down at your right and left hand, and talking across you, for an hour, over their private and utterly trivial concerns.

In a coffee house, on shaking off a long reverie, the sudden consciousness that, during the whole of your absent fit, your eyes have been intently fixed on a letter that a stranger is writing or reading at your elbow.

While on a short visit to town — the hurry and ferment, the crossing and jostling, the missing and marring, which incessantly happen among all your engagements, purposes and promises; both of business and

pleasure, at home and abroad, from morning till midnight: obstacles equally perverse, unexpected, unaccountable, innumerable and intolerable, springing up like mushrooms through every step of your progress.

In going out of town, being met and blockaded on the road by innumerable gangs of the carrion and offal of the human species swarming home, in savage jollity, from a bull-baiting, a boxing match, an execution or a similar game or sport.

A bad Sunday in the City.

Miseries
of
Watering
Places

51

Watering places! — a mighty soft name truly for a parcel of pest-houses, which you visit for the express convenience of being ducked like a thief a dozen times in a week, and then, by way of recovering your breath, toiling up one perpendicular cliff and down another.

Timothy Testy

On arriving at a poor watering place in the dark, finding, from some mischief among your previous arrangements, no lodging prepared: then, groping your way to the inn — as the only hole in which you can pig for the night; with the exhilarating prospect before you of pigging there again the night following and, indeed, as many nights more as you choose to stay in the place; having just learned that every house, and part of a house, is already seized for three months certain; and, on the departure of the present set, for three months more!

Running away from your own Palace in Paradise, for the sake of hiring a thin slice of a tall, crazy, toy-house, looking out, at the back, on a dry desert, and in front on a wet one. Your share of the space consisting, in all, of one closet to sit up in, and another to lie down in; with a fair chance of being carried into the sea, house and all, by the first puff of wind that may favour the launch; all these advantages having been obtained, with great trouble and difficulty, at the rate of twenty guineas a week.

Sauntering day by day, at the same hours, along the same cliff or beach, till it is time to visit the same library, coffee shop or alehouse, there to see the same idiots yawning in each other's faces at the sound of each other's voices; many of them, moreover, having a claim on you for a nod and forced simper, as often as you meet them — the only mitigation of your misery being that when you have once escaped from the place, you shall never hear of them again.

Learning to swim for the first time, i.e. being soused and smothered fifty times in a minute, with a view to acquiring the accomplishment of kicking and sprawling like a frog (only not half so well), along the top of the water for a few yards, without going to the bottom.

After going down to the beach, lingering and shivering about the sands for an hour till you can snatch courage to make your own attempt to be drowned, with a choice of pitching yourself headlong into the raging deep, or crawling down the steps and making a low bow to the first wave that you can catch in the humour to swallow you up and wreck your breathless carcase against the shore. Then, on regaining land in your new character (that of a bruised and bleeding cripple), you discover that your towel is safely locked up at home.

When unable to dry yourself properly after bathing, *screwing on* your clinging clothes.

Going to a seaside raffle, which (unless you have the good luck to lose), encumbers you with a prize made up of fifty trumpery toys, not one of which you can contrive to be glad of.

53

Ploughing, knee-deep in sand, shells or pebbles, for a whole morning together, to grub for marine curiosities, which you do not find.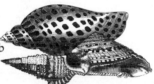

While pensively standing on a slippery crag upon the beach, to watch the return of the tide, in full confidence of the firmness of your footing — to be suddenly undeceived as to this latter, particularly by an overgrown *tenth wave*, as it trips you up and then walks over you at leisure.

In walking on the cliff — to be frightened to death twenty times in the course of your walk by the heroic frolics of the young men of your party, who make a rule of approaching nearer to the precipice the more loudly you scream out your entreaties that they would keep away.

On the morning after entering your name in the book of arrivals, perceiving with astonishment that, wherever you appear, you are the mark of general whispers, accompanied with a sort of curiosity equally pointed and unflattering, till, at the moment of your departure, the mystery is unveiled by the casual discovery of the truth — that you are indebted for this singular reception to the accident of bearing both the Christian and surname of the most notorious murderer in the country.

At a forlorn bathing place, listlessly wandering from one poor shop to another, with an indeterminate desire to purchase something, just by way of feeling yourself to be alive; and finding yourself in the dilemma of keeping your money burning in your pocket, or of buying a variety of articles, which you could not want, even if they were worth a halfpenny.

At the seaside, dragging one leg after another up and down the strand as long as you can stand it, because other people drag theirs in like manner, because *exercise* is good after bathing, because you *may* spy out the face of an old acquaintance among your fellow prisoners, and because, bad as it all is, anything is better than returning through the dirty alleys to the blank room of your hovel in the suburbs for the purpose of yawning over a bad novel during the rest of the day.

The absolute famine of all mental entertainment that distinguishes any watering place, added to the drowsiness brought on by bathing, ingrafted upon the natural dullness of the place.

Going to bed awake, in perfect health, between nine and ten o'clock, because your friends are invalids or valetudinarians; or because you must all get up to be thrown into the sea soon after daybreak.

Miseries of Fashionable Life

What are theatres, but licensed repositories for ill-told lies, or stifling shambles for the voluntary sacrifice of time, health, money and morals?

Samuel Sensitive

At a July party — to be locked up in the very heart of the most crowded of all the rooms, by an elegant jam of the human kind — closely bounded, at your right, left, front and rear, by a *quaternion* of dull Dowagers for whose ears you have to furnish nonsense in rotation, during the whole term of your confinement. And this while you are doubly tantalized: first, by catching an occasional glimpse of your Inamorata at an inaccessible distance; next, by seeing various salvers of cooling refreshments perpetually coasting round the mass of the company, of which you, in all the rage of heat, thirst and vexation, are the motionless centre. To complete your destruction, not only is every window hermetically sealed down, but, in compassion to the bones of a few crazy Countesses, there is a blazing fire.

56   The endless interval while you are sitting by a lady, whom you consider it your duty to entertain, but who does not consider it as *her* duty to be entertained.

The laborious necessity of going every night to see your *friends*, at full speed, between the hours of ten o'clock at night and five or six o'clock the next morning — the humour of the thing lying altogether in being able to count over upon your fingers a greater number of drawing rooms and clubs into which you can prove that you have popped, in the above interval, than the rest of their Graces and their Ladyships can do.

A variety of tantalizing entertainments cruelly falling on the same night — so that for want of the convenient attribute of ubiquity you are condemned to a sickly, unsatisfied relish of the present object, by a tormenting anxiety to be in a dozen other places.

On your own night 'at home', the counter-attraction of a rival party operating so powerfully against you that your visitors are barely numerous enough to stuff your suite of rooms — leaving the *staircase* almost entirely unpeopled.

The joys of a *fête-champêtre*! After you have duly crowded all your walks, lawns and shrubberies with more company, and covered your tables with more delicacies than either can conveniently hold, the whole apparatus of enchantment washed away in an instant by an impolite deluge of rain.

Going, with ardent expectations, to a picnic, and finding that, from some sudden capriccio in the decrees of fashion, there is no *nic* to *pick*.

Going to the theatre on a very crowded night, waiting an hour in the pit passage, half jammed to death, receiving a dreadful kick on the ankle, and, in making a desperate effort to stoop down to rub it, finding your hand in the coat pocket of the man who stands opposite you, and gradually withdrawing it with indescribable horror, so as just to escape being taken for a pickpocket.

In the pit, at the opera, a broad-shouldered fellow, seven feet high, seated immediately before you, during the whole of the ballet.

On going to the play to see a favourite performer, to be told, at the drawing up of the curtain (as you had augured from the rueful bow of the speaker), that he, or she, is suddenly taken ill, or dead, and that Mr ... or Miss   (the hacks of the house) has kindly undertaken to try to read the part at five minutes' notice.

While sitting in the front row of the front boxes, during the deepest part of the tragedy, yourself and your friends suddenly required to stand up and crowd back upon each other, while you hold up the seat for a large party in procession, who take up twenty minutes in getting down to their places, in one of which you had seated yourself by mistake, and consequently are now turned out, and have to tread back your way to the lobby, over the laps of ladies, without a chance for another seat.

Your opera-glass (which had been perfectly clear while there was nothing in the house worth spying at), becoming obstinately dim at the moment when you have pointed it towards an enchanting creature who has just entered.

58

Sitting, with an excruciating headache, to see a vile play, acted by viler performers, for the eighth or tenth time, in a crowded back row of a little theatre, with a dull party, in August.

Wading through the gossiping scenes of the play, in which the lackeys and maids lay their heads together about the characters of their masters and mistresses, knowing that all this while the chief actors are refreshing themselves and relaxing behind the scenes.

At a pantomime, when the entry of the devils is announced by a discordant crash of the instruments, being told by a man near you that he thinks *the orchestra not quite in tune.*

At the theatre, the loss of your delight in looking at the faces and figures of the female performers, after the enchantment has been dissolved by a closer inspection behind the scenes.

Just as you are beginning to recover yourself, after a song of unequalled length and insipidity — "encore! encore!" — from every mouth in the house except your own, which is fully taken up with hissing and yawning, alternately.

Attending private theatricals where the gentlemen performers always press near the prompter's side, always hurry over passages in order to catch every word before it slips from the memory, one performer not giving the cue word, or giving it, and it not being remembered by the other who plays with him; both standing like posts when they have nothing to say, and using their legs and arms as if they had just been bestowed upon them.

Going to the Exhibition at so exquisitely late an hour as, you fondly flatter yourself, will completely shelter you from the riff-raff: till, on entering the Great Room, you split at once on the discovery that you have waited till the turn of the tide; all the people whom it is possible to look at having just retired, and left you gasping with horror, amidst a fry of wretches, who have shoaled from all the unheard-of holes of the City and Suburbs. **59**

A bad Exhibition! Being obliged to admire a painting that is but a lurid whirl of miscellaneous monstrosities — this obscure and turbid fermentation of floundering abortions, which would seem to be inhabited by beings — or rather, ambiguous and reserved innuendoes of beings — fluctuating somewhere among the shadowy and unsettled nomenclatures of incantation, demon, wizard, griffin, goblin, &c., &c.

After the opera — your carriage having been mutilated in the wars of the coachmen, and all your friends having driven away — the hideous possibility of being reduced to steal off in that grave of delicacy, a hackney coach!

Being a lady of a certain age, throwing yourself into your carriage at daybreak, after some long and fatiguing orgy, finding yourself face to face with your gentleman escort, with the killing consciousness that the beams of the rising sun, by pointing at certain little derangements in the composition of your countenance, are gradually rectifying a few chronological errors in your own history, into which you had been leading him an hour before.

While you are rolling, at the proper hour of the day, through the proper streets of the town, in your new carriage — with the equally malicious and delicious project of dazzling and mortifying every competitor — to find, as you examine the passing equipages, that you are at least a fortnight behind the newest Leader.

(Note: At this time, Leader were the only makers in whoses carriages the bones of the Beau Monde were considered as out of danger.)

60

At the card-table — in a humdrum house, at which you are sometimes condemned to murder an evening — playing for nothing, when accustomed to the excitement of risking half your fortune.

At the casino — in rising from the table after a whole night passed in losing one deep stake after another — the sardonic grin that you feel to have substituted itself for the easy smile you intended.

The awkward recollection that sometimes flits across you — as you are spiritedly staking a few loose thousands at a casino, paying for half a dozen *chef-d'œuvres* at a picture-sale, &c. — that you are, at the same time, throwing a harmless shopkeeper into jail for life, breaking his wife's heart, and starving all his children.

Spending your days in one of those mausoleums of the living, a stately home, and losing yourself in the dim cells, howling halls, forbidden chambers, forgotten garrets, interminable galleries and labyrinths of the immemorial pile.

Miseries of Reading and Writing

What are society and solitude, but, each, an alternative hiding place from the persecutions of the other? Libraries! What are they but the sepulchres of gaiety, or conservatories for the seedlings of disease?

Samuel Sensitive

Reading over a passage in an author, for the hundredth time, without coming an inch nearer to the meaning of it; then passing over it in despair, but without being able to enjoy the rest of the book, from the painful consciousness of your own real or supposed stupidity.

Reading newspaper poetry, which, by a sort of fatality that you can neither explain nor resist, you occasionally slave through, in the midst of the utmost repugnance and disgust.

Straining your eyes over a book in the twilight, at the rate of about five minutes per line, before it occurs to you to obtain some light.

62 **T**oiling through a novel seven or eight volumes long ... with this exquisite addition to your woes, that, when you have at last forced through it, you have become perfectly satisfied of a dreadful fact that you had more than once suspected in the course of the book: that you had read it before!

While sitting up all alone, through the whole of a damp, chill, joyless night, over a book that you are anxious to finish — the increasing sense of nervous, shivering, desolate anxiety, sharpened with self-reproach, which comes over you towards three or four o'clock in the morning.

The joys of reading in bed in the Winter, i.e. overlaying one of your arms till it is cramped, and exposing the other till it is frostbitten ... with the *relief*, however, of perpetually shifting from one uneasy posture to another, for the advantage either of fumbling over the leaf, snuffing your dim light, or preventing the partial eclipse occasioned by the intervention of that opaque item, your head, from becoming total.

Reading a favourite book from the Library, which has, *very obviously*, passed through the unwashed hands of all the subscribers.

While very poor, and likely to remain so, the tantalizing task you have imposed on yourself of continually adding to your visionary catalogue of the books to be bought when rich.

After having sent from the other end of the kingdom for a quantity of well-chosen books, all particularly named — receiving in return, six months afterwards, a cargo of novels, with such titles as *Delicate Sensibility, Disguises of the Heart, Errors of Tenderness* and so forth. Then, if you venture, in despair, on a few pages, being edified in the margin by such pencilled commentaries as the following: "I quite agree with this sentiment."; "How frequently do we find this to be the case in real life!"; "But why did she let him have the letter?", &c., &c.

63

Continuing to read long after your memory is clogged, and your attention jaded, merely because you have nothing else to do.

In reading a book of travels — viewing through another's eyes the most exquisite scenes, which you are physically certain that you shall never see with your own.

Reading in a fluttering current of air, which every instant saves you the trouble of turning the pages.

Trying to read a letter in which the handwriting is elegant rather than legible; the letters being delicately, and, as it were, accidentally dropped from the pen.

Looking for a good pen (which it is your perverse destiny never to find, except when you are indifferent about it).

Writing upon a thin sheet of paper with very small crumbs of bread under it. Or, writing a long letter, with a very hard pen, on very thin and very greasy paper, with very pale ink, to someone you dislike.

Writing at the top of a very long sheet of paper; so that you either rumple and crease the lower end of it with your arm against the table, in bringing it lower down, or bruise your chest and drive out all your breath, in stretching forward to the upper end.

64

Attempting to erase a mistake, but, in fact, only scratching holes in the paper.

Hearing an ode of your own composition, which you think pregnant with Pindaric fire and sublimity, called "pretty".

Suddenly finding, safe in your pocket, three or four letters of the most pressing consequence, entrusted to your care a week or fortnight before, by a person hardly known to you, upon the faith of your promise to put them into the post within an hour.

Borrowing, on condition of returning it tomorrow morning, a book consisting almost wholly of short, detached phrases such as: "The Miseries of Human Life."

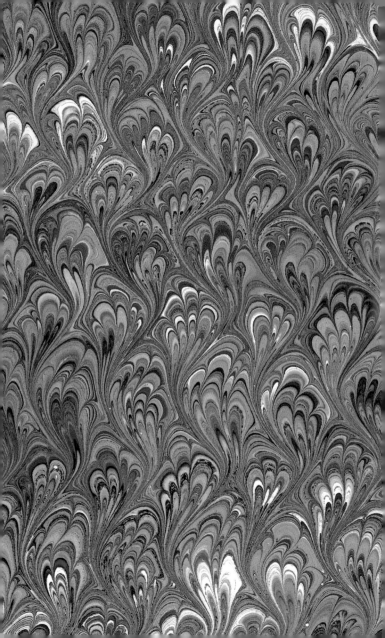